A PO

THE

OF
EVERYTHING

Copyright

ISBN 978-0995620285

Preface

The hope for A Poetic Theory Of Everything is to:

- Introduce you to areas of science such as Quantum Mechanics that are not commonly taught in depth in schools.
- To arouse your curiosity in the wonders of our Universe.
- To encourage you to be ambitious and develop a keen interest in furthering your education on a broad range of scientific topics.
- To inspire you to consider future employment within the scientific community in areas such as *Theoretical Physics* and *Astrophysics*.

A Poetic Theory Of Everything is suitable for people aged ten years and upwards.

Poems vary in complexity and are packed full of references for you to research and explore further.

There are 34 poems included in this book.

According to Wikipedia:

34 is one of the new magic numbers in physics.

Quote from Wikipedia:

'In nuclear physics, a magic number is a number of nucleons (either protons or neutrons separately) such that they are arranged into complete shells within the atomic nucleus.'

34 is also the magic constant of a 4 by 4 normal magic square in mathematics.

Contents

A Theory Of Everything

I combine *General Relativity* with *Quantum Mechanics*,
The latter can seem spooky and eerie,
You need me to explain all physical aspects of your Universe,
Because I am the all-encompassing master theory.

Until my unification has been discovered,
You will have no explanation,
As to what happened in the first moments,
Of your Universe's creation.

Quantum Mechanics describes,
The behaviour of your sub-microscopic world,
And Einstein's theory of General Relativity explains,
The gravitational pull in which you are held.

Mass warps the fabric of *spacetime*,
So, Relativity says *gravity* is not a force at all,
But you wonder if it can be quantised,
On a scale that is infinitesimally small.

Bridging the gap between *gravity* and the forces of nature,
Would give physicists satisfaction,
I am a set of fundamental principles,
Unifying gravity with the *electronuclear interaction*.

I can explain all physical phenomena,
With a much deeper understanding,
Of how *Weak* and *Strong forces* merge,
Providing you with a *Theory Of Everything*.

I am the part of your Universe,
That keeps secrets locked away,
But perhaps scientists will find the answers,
That you are hoping for some day.

Fundamental Forces And Quarks

They are much smaller than atoms,
They are subatomic particles,
You can read about them,
In many academic articles.

Bosons and *fermions* are,
The groups that they are placed in,
Bosons have a *spin* of 0, 1, 2, 3 and more,
And fermions have a *half-integer spin*.

Wavefunctions of bosons such as,
Higgs, photons, gluons and *W* and *Z*,
Are unlike fermions with *antisymmetric wavefunctions*,
Because they have *symmetric wavefunctions* instead.

Gravity is a force due to the curvature of spacetime,
To the Earth gravitational forces keep us glued,
Gravitons are the hypothetical quantum of gravity,
This is the force the *Standard Model* does not include.

The *electromagnetic force* is carried by photons,
Gluons are responsible for the *Strong nuclear interaction*,
The *Weak nuclear force* is carried by the W and Z bosons,
The fourth force of nature is the gravitational attraction.

Gauge bosons in the Standard Model,
Are the three force-carrying particles in particle physics,
And the twelve particles of matter,
Are fermions divided into two sets of six.

One set are the six *quark flavours*,
Each named well enough not to be forgotten,
There's *Up*, *Down*, *Strange* and *Charm*,
And there's also *Top* and *Bottom*.

Two Up quarks and one Down make a *proton*,
The Strong interaction is how nucleons are bound,
A *neutron* has two Down quarks and one Up,
Inside an atom's nucleus is where they are found.

Electrically neutral *electron neutrinos*, *muon neutrinos*,
And *tau neutrinos* are half of the set of *leptons*,
The other half are electrically charged muons,
And tau particles and *electrons*.

Helium Atom

If you could see our atom,
Because we could be enlarged,
You would see two electrons orbiting us,
In a cloud that is negatively charged.

We exist inside the nucleus,
Bunched up inside the core,
Similar to us in mass are neutrons,
Together we make four.

We have a positive electrical charge,
Protons are our name,
Neutrons contain quarks just like us,
But we are not the same.

One Up quark and two Down for the neutrons,
One Down and two Up for us,
Opposites attract so we repel,
With our positive *plus plus*.

With great force from within the nucleus,
We would push each other away,
At thousands of miles per second,
If the Strong nuclear force didn't make us stay.

The Strong nuclear force counteracts,
The *electromagnetic repulsion*,
Holding us and the neutrons together,
And so, avoiding our expulsion.

The gluon is a massless gauge boson,
Each force has a gauge boson of its own,
The gluon carries the Strong interaction,
Which within short range is the strongest force known!

Casimir Effect And Dynamical Casimir Effect

We are called *virtual particles*,
Because straight after we are created,
Inside the *vacuum of Space*,
We are immediately *annihilated.*

Two uncharged conductive plates,
Placed closely together in a vacuum,
About a micrometre apart,
Did not give us photons much room.

Some of us were trapped inside the gap,
Where photons with long wavelengths could not fit,
More of us were created on the outside,
Of the plates that we hit.

The pressure exerted on the outside,
Of each metal plate,
Pushed them together,
Because the force was so great.

Theoretical Physicists found too many,
Huge infinities in each complex calculation,
So, they avoided this mathematical problem,
By using a process called *renormalization.*

When Physicists accelerated the plates back and forth,
I lost my partner and became real,
But the first law of *thermodynamics* was not violated,
So, *conservation of energy* meant there was nothing to steal.

Electron

You are a proton and I am an electron,
You are positive and locked in place,
Your elementary charge is plus one,
Mine is minus one and I can leap through Space.

You may at times be,
Uncertain of my exact location,
Want to give me up,
Or share me with another creation.

My existence was unknown,
Until 1879 on a very special day,
When J. J. Thomson observed me in a vacuum tube,
As an electron stream called a *cathode ray*.

George Johnstone Stoney named me,
I have zero dimensions,
I am a *pointlike particle*,
Lacking spatial extension.

Quarks and gluons are your building blocks,
You can temporarily convert the latter,
Into quark and antiquark pairs of which,
Quarks are the fundamental constituent of matter.

They use equations called *Quantum Chromodynamics,*
To describe your quarks' colour, charge and force interaction,
Your proton number is the same as my electron number,
In a neutral atom and our opposite charges are a strong attraction.

Some like me were once *gamma ray photons*,
Travelling at the speed of light anywhere,
Until they interacted with the magnetic field,
And converted into an electron and *positron* pair.

The positron’s opposite charge to mine,
Means that we spin in the opposite direction,
This is how Physicists can confirm,
An *antimatter* particle detection.

When I am in atomic orbitals,
I often drop down to my ground state,
And if a positron should touch me,
Then we will annihilate.

When you and I collide, we cause *electron capture*,
You absorb me from your inner atomic shell,
If you collide with another proton creating a W boson,
It will decay creating more of me and neutrinos as well.

You are a b*aryon* and I am a lepton,
Quarks were found through our *Deep Inelastic Scatter*,
You and I along with neutrons,
Make up the basic building blocks of ordinary matter.

Quantum Entanglement

Our mysterious particles,
Have become attracted,
Our wavefunction has entangled,
Since we last interacted.

Now linked in such a way,
That whatever we do,
You can affect me,
And I can affect you.

We exist inside the same Universe,
That the humans live,
But they find us bizarre,
And counterintuitive.

My spin points to the left,
We have no sound, smell or sight,
But still somehow you know,
And your spin points to the right.

Our quantum connection,
Through language unspoken,
Goes unseen and unknown,
So is therefore unbroken.

In this spooky state,
We shall remain perhaps,
Until a curious observer,
Causes our wavefunction to collapse!

Refraction

Electron got himself,
Into a fight,
Claiming that he,
Could travel faster than Light.

Electron dared Light,
To race him in a swimming pool,
Light agreed with confidence,
And called Electron "a fool".

They both raced through the water,
After shooting through the air,
When Electron took the lead,
Light exclaimed, "this isn't fair!"

In physics, Electron explained to Light,
It is wrong to just assume,
That you can propagate fastest in any medium,
As well as in a vacuum!

The race was close but Electron won,
And Light regretted being dared,
But Light pointed out to Electron,
That E still equals mc squared!

Quantum Field Theory (QFT)

A particle in *Quantum Field Theory*,
Is an excitation of its Quantum Field,
These fields exist throughout our Universe,
Although imperceptibly concealed.

Inside the *Large Hadron Collider*,
Which continues to amaze and astound,
In Geneva, on July the fourth 2012,
The *Higgs boson* was finally found.

Energy fields interact with each other,
Elementary particles are their vibrations,
So, in the Standard Model the Higgs boson,
Is produced by its *Higgs field* excitation.

The Higgs Field has its own,
Intrinsic interaction rules,
Reacting a lot more with,
Only certain particles.

Quarks and Leptons,
Physicists have explained,
Are passing through the Higgs Field,
And as a result, more mass is gained.

When W and Z bosons, Higgs and,
Top quarks interacted with this Field a lot,
Physicists' calculations revealed,
The heavier those particles got!

So, the W and Z bosons are among,
The heaviest particles of course,
They are much more massive than the proton,
And they are known as the Weak Force.

Electrons also interact with the Higgs Field,
Even though they are so small,
Whereas massless particles like Photons,
Do not interact at all!

Young's Double Slit Experiment

Shoot me through your slits,
For I am brave,
I will astound you with,
My goodbye wave!

One shot at a time,
Was your cunning decision,
To rule out the possibility,
Of any particle collision.

When my peaks and troughs overlapped,
They formed a dark pattern of destructive interference,
When they lined up, they formed a constructive one,
Which was of a light appearance.

So, fire away!
Can you not see?
It is all based,
On probability!

Doppler Effect – Lightwaves And Cosmological Redshift

There are colours of light wave frequencies,
That my human eyes have missed,
They can see only parts of the *electromagnetic spectrum*,
But so many more exist.

Ranging from the lowest frequency and energy,
At the *longwave* end where photons appear as red,
To the highest frequency and energy at the *shortwave* end,
Where they appear as blue instead.

From the longwave end of the spectrum are:
Radio waves, microwaves, infrared and visible light,
Ultraviolet, X-rays and gamma rays of which,
Only the fourth in line can be detected by human eyesight.

The Doppler effect can be seen by using a Spectroscope,
Separating each wave with its different frequency.
Compressed *blueshifted* light is moving in my direction,
And stretched *redshifted* light is moving away from me.

The *Cosmological Redshift* is one of the ways,
Cosmologists have proven that the Universe is expanding,
Supporting the theory of the *Big Bang*,
And increasing human understanding.

Doppler Effect – Water Waves
Mermaid Style

She is a particle Mermaid,
Rather strangely she behaves,
With two sides to her nature,
She swims in particle waves.

You become perplexed as she exhibits,
Her *wave-particle duality*,
But like light and sound that's all around,
She is the very nature of reality!

When she shoots her tiny bits of matter,
Through a slit onto the wall behind,
One single band of particles,
Is all that you will find.

When a second slit is added,
An interference pattern shows,
But observation collapses the wavefunction,
So, into the water the Mermaid goes.

Your understanding of her,
Becomes a challenge to grip,
As she passes through a slit between,
The timbers of a half sunken ship.

You observe her two waves as they collide,
And pass straight through each other,
You see them cancel themselves out,
When one is on top of another.

You want to learn more,
Because her properties intrigue you,
So, you set up an experiment,
To see what she will do.

Her forward moving waves,
Join together in a single collection,
One passes through the slit alone,
Before spreading out in every direction.

You then widen the slit,
To remove any doubt,
That her waves flowing to the sides,
Will cancel each other out.

You watch her forward-moving waves,
Travelling one after another,
Wave after wave,
As they strengthen each other.

You further widen the slit,
Between the timber sections,
Strengthening her waves,
In all directions.

When her wave peaks become larger than you,
Your body she passes around.
There's a larger distance between her wave peaks,
Than most objects in the case of sound.

She now becomes smaller than you,
Between her points of peak distance,
You block her waves as you ponder,
The complexity of her very existence.

Doppler Effect – Sound Waves

The source of the sound was a moving police car,
On which a loud siren was fitted,
A nearby observer heard,
The sound that was being emitted.

As the siren approached the observer,
The pitch sounded unchanged for the police,
But the frequency that the observer was detecting,
Began to intensify and increase.

As the car moved further away,
The observer heard another change in sound,
The frequency and pitch were lower,
Because the soundwaves had spread out all around.

The LHC

The *Large Hadron Collider*,
In Geneva, Switzerland at CERN,
Was designed by Engineers and Mathematicians,
So that Scientists can learn.

About subatomic particles like,
muons, neutrinos and pions,
By smashing protons together,
With heavy lead ions.

It has two beam pipes,
In two separate tube sections,
Kept at ultrahigh vacuum,
Protons move in opposite directions.

The beams of accelerated particles,
Are kept narrow and tight,
Travelling at about one millionth of a percent,
Slower than the speed of light.

Approximately every 25 nanoseconds,
While particles are zooming around,
A collision takes place,
That's how the Higgs boson was found.

Curvature of the scattering,
Gives Physicists useful information,
To help improve human understanding,
Of our Universe's creation.

Facts And Figures

3.14159 is an approximation of,
The mathematical constant, *Pi*.
It has been estimated that 5,000 stars,
Can be seen with the naked eye.

The Fibonacci number sequence,
Starts with 0,1,1,2,3,5,8,13,
Many people want to walk on the moon,
But only 12 have been.

There are 3,600 seconds in an hour,
And 86,400 seconds in one day.
On the 14th of March 1879, Einstein was born,
That date in 2018, Stephen Hawking passed away.

5.88 trillion miles is roughly,
The equivalent of one lightyear.
Proxima Centauri b is an Earth-like planet,
Approximately 4.2 lightyears away from here.

The Universe has existed,
For 14 billion years, since its creation,
And *cosmic background* is the oldest,
Electromagnetic radiation.

Stars orbit at approximately 230 kilometres per second,
At varied distances from the galactic centre of the *Milky Way*,
And more than 2.5 quintillion bytes of data,
Are being created every day.

Heisenberg's Uncertainty Principle Equation $\Delta x \Delta p \geq h/4\pi$

In this equation *Delta* is,
Symbolised as a triangle,
It is used to refer to the *uncertainty*,
Of both the *x* and *p variables*.

Delta p and *Delta x* are the uncertainty,
Of the particle's *momentum* and *position*,
We cannot know both at the same time,
With accurate precision.

Delta x multiplied by Delta p,
Is greater than or equal to h over 4 pi.
Planck's constant is a tiny quantity represented by the h,
And 12.6 is approximately what it is divided by.

As the uncertainty in either x or p rises,
The uncertainty in the other will fall,
This is the relationship between position,
And momentum in the *Uncertainty Principle*.

Great Minds

On July the 20th, 1969 *Neil Armstrong*,
And *Buzz Aldrin* achieved the first moon landing.
Scientific breakthroughs about how our Universe behaves,
Offers humanity a much deeper understanding.

Albert Einstein was a theoretical physicist,
Remembered for his equation $E=mc^2$,
Well known for being a genius,
As well as eccentric and wild-haired.

Special Relativity explains the motion of objects,
With respect to each other in every *inertial reference frame*,
And how the speed of light within a vacuum,
Is independent for observers and remains the same.

Einstein married his first cousin Elsa,
After his first marriage ended in divorce,
His *Thought Experiments* gave us General Relativity,
Which explains our perception of gravity as a force.

Stephen Hawking was a theoretical physicist and cosmologist,
Fathering three children and marrying twice,
Eventually wheelchair-bound with Motor Neurone Disease,
He communicated through a speech-generating device.

Stephen tackled complex scientific concepts,
Theorising the possible destruction of information,
Trapped in circular orbits inside *Black Holes*,
That emit *Hawking Radiation*.

He presented a theory to resolve the information paradox,
He published many books as well,
Such as *A Brief History Of Time*,
And *The Universe In A Nutshell*.

With his explanation of the origin of our Universe,
Our understanding still grows,
He wrote theorems on *gravitational singularity*,
In his collaboration with *Sir Roger Penrose*.

Of the *Minkowski Diagram*,
Roger's *Penrose Diagram* is an extension,
Illustrating causal relations between different points,
In spacetime using two dimensions.

Roger is a mathematical physicist who proposed,
Twistor Theory, where twistor space is *chiral*,
And mathematician *Leonardo Fibonacci* is famous for,
His work on *Fibonacci numbers* and the *Fibonacci spiral*.

Richard Feynman was a theoretical physicist who worked,
On the path integral formulation of Quantum Mechanics,
And the superfluidity of supercooled liquid helium,
Sharing a Nobel Prize for his theory of *Quantum Electrodynamics*.

Erwin Schrödinger is known for his Schrödinger's cat,
It is an analogy based on the *Copenhagen Interpretation*,
And English theoretical physicist *Paul Dirac*,
Was the first to predict *antimatter* creation.

In 2019 computer scientist, *Katherine Louise Bouman*,
Led a team that developed an algorithm for imaging Black Holes,
Analysing these images to learn more about General Relativity,
In a strong gravitational field, are Katie and her team's goals.

Our understanding of atomic structure,
Has been increased, thanks to the physicist *Niels Bohr*.
And *Nikola Tesla* dreamed of a world with free energy,
Each person a genius and there are so many more!

The Macroscopic

Our solar system is contained,
By our galaxy, the Milky Way,
And our planet's rotation is slowing,
Extending the length of each Earth day.

There are eight planets from our Sun,
The first four are Mercury, Venus, Earth and Mars.
It has been estimated that the Milky Way galaxy
Contains up to 400 billion stars.

The next four planets in line are,
Jupiter, Saturn, Uranus and Neptune.
Our Earth orbits the Sun,
And is itself orbited by our moon.

Although the Universe is expanding,
At an increasingly rapid speed,
The Milky Way and *Andromeda* are set to collide,
As most other galaxies recede.

The accelerating expansion of the Universe,
Exceeds the speed of light,
But no information is carried with it,
So Special Relativity is still right!

If a particle could travel faster than light speed,
It would make 'time reversal' a reality,
But an *effect* cannot occur before its *cause* because,
That would violate the laws of physics and *causality*.

Our Sun

At the centre of our solar system,
Is our planet's closest star,
Necessary for the existence of life on Earth,
It's our most important energy source by far.

At *solar maximum* many dark patches,
Known as *sunspots* temporarily appear,
They are cooler than the rest,
Of the Sun's photosphere.

Stars are comprised of plasma,
They are almost perfect spheres,
Our Sun's eleven-year sunspot cycle is a part,
Of its solar activity of twenty-two years.

For the first half the Sun's *Northern Hemisphere*,
Is where the magnetic north can be found,
And the magnetic south is in the *Southern Hemisphere*,
Until the *magnetic fields* get flipped around.

This reversal of polarity includes,
Changes in the levels of *solar radiation*,
As the number and size of sunspots increase,
So do *solar flares* and other manifestations.

Moving from the Sun's mid-latitudes,
Solar minimum begins in the eleventh year,
Sunspots become fewer, moving closer to the Equator,
And can affect Earth's atmosphere.

Death Of A Star

My big celestial brother,
Once lit up your nights,
Filling the skies,
With twinkling lights.

He was not only a star,
He was also my friend,
Until a *supernova* explosion,
Brought his life to an end.

As his electrons repelled,
I wondered if perhaps,
Electron degeneracy pressure,
Would avert his core collapse.

But he had run out of fuel,
And the pressure was so great,
That a giant nucleus,
Was his stellar remnant's fate.

His powerful *gravity*,
Compressed him immensely,
His protons and electrons combined into neutrons,
As they smashed together intensely.

He became a planet-like star,
With an outer crust of his own,
And a magnetic field,
With a strength that had grown.

He was so much smaller,
Compared to what he was at the start,
And *neutron degenerative pressure*,
Stopped him from falling apart.

His density was so extreme,
And his neutrons were squashed so tightly,
That he almost broke *Pauli's Exclusion Principle*,
Because they were overlapping slightly.

I once observed his zombie corpse,
The light from his radiating *pulsar* is how,
And I often wonder if perhaps,
He is an exotic *quark star* now.

Information Paradox

An entangled copy of my story,
Fell into a Black Hole in Space,
Shredding my words into letters,
Inside an unreachable place.

The *Apparent Horizon*,
Had already been crossed,
I was unsure if my copy,
Was forever lost.

I wondered if aeons later,
A *Firewall* burned,
And if my jumbled-up letters,
Would ever be returned.

Event Horizon or Apparent?
Perhaps in a long time or never,
My letters and words,
Might be put back together.

Life as we know it

The *Cambrian explosion*,
Followed a colossal cataclysm,
Bacteria provided the oxygen,
For each multicellular organism.

For at least 3.5 billion years,
Life on Earth has been evolving,
Rotating on its axis,
While around the Sun you are revolving.

Your Sun and solar system,
Are also revolving away,
At 230 kilometres per second,
Around the centre of your galaxy the Milky Way.

Carbon atoms in the heart of a dying star,
Recycle organic material into something new,
Therefore, you are just as much a part of the Universe,
As the Universe is a part of you!

Aliens On Earth

Does the *Bombardier Beetle* have you questioning,
Darwin's theory of evolution?
With its chemical reaction defence mechanism,
Of a hydroquinone and hydrogen peroxide solution.

And have you ever wondered why the *Tuatara reptile*,
Has a third eye with a retina, lens and cornea on its head?
Or how it has survived the Middle Triassic Period,
When all the Dinosaurs are dead?

Or why the blue-blooded *Octopus* has three hearts,
And an advanced cognition that allows it to play?
Or how its blood is copper-based and it has neurons in each arm,
And the ability to routinely edit its own *RNA*?

Have you puzzled over the microscopic *Tardigrade*,
And its resilience to extreme temperatures and dehydration?
Or its ability to survive in the vacuum of Space?
And exposure to extremely high and low pressures and radiation?

Eyes of some species of the *Mantis shrimp*,
Have twelve different *photoreceptor types* or more,
Unlike the visual pigments of human beings,
Who are limited to only four!

The fascinating attributes of the Mantis Shrimp,
Do not end with their incredible sight,
They also create a phenomenon called *sonoluminescence*,
By snapping their claws, they produce scorching bubbles of light.

Do you realise the importance of bees pollinating flowers?
And the probability of their death with every sting?
If there's one thing that we can know with certainty it is...
That nature is a wonderful thing!

Zero The Hero

You plunge to the depths,
Of the temperature scale,
Where such extreme cold,
Is considered the Holy Grail!

The third law of thermodynamics,
Needs a brave superhero,
To explain the *entropy* of a system,
When it reaches almost *absolute zero*!

You are cooler than below one *nanokelvin*,
As you fight an *information deception* crime,
Because you know that a particle's position and momentum,
Cannot be measured at exactly the same time!

You inform the world that at -273.15 °C,
Moving particles do not stop dead,
As the Heisenberg Uncertainty Principle,
Means that they are vibrating instead!

Waves form and matter becomes,
More ordered as temperatures fall,
But these strange quantum effects,
Do not faze you at all!

Because you are a *zero-point* superhero!
And science is relying on you.
For things like particle accelerators, quantum computers,
And MRI machines to name just a few!

Light

At 186,282 miles per second,
I can travel from Earth to the Sun.
In just 8 minutes and 20 seconds,
My journey is already done.

If mankind matches my speed,
And somehow survives,
A whole Universe they could see,
In their transient lives.

I am needed for *photosynthesis*,
Because oxygen is imperative,
For all *aerobic life* on Earth,
To continue to live.

I am known to *refract*,
Whenever I pass,
From one medium to another,
Such as water or glass.

There are parts of my spectrum,
That humans cannot see,
The Doppler effect is used to measure,
The speed of each star and galaxy.

I have wave-particle duality,
I cannot be blocked by magnetic shields,
My path can be altered,
By large gravitational fields.

I interact with matter,
I am a part of electromagnetic radiation,
I have been around since,
The very first moment of creation.

I am carried by photons which are,
The elementary particles you need for sight,
Only hypothetical particles can travel faster than me,
I am what illuminates your world. I am light!

Dark Matter

You are less than five percent of this Universe,
You are *baryonic matter*,
85% of the total mass-energy is *dark*,
Of which I am the latter.

I have no electrical charge,
I cannot be detected by sight,
Find me by using gravitational lensing,
In high concentrations I bend light.

Galaxy clusters form where my filaments meet,
Bending light makes their mass possible to find,
This should theoretically also map their location,
By the distortion of the objects behind.

I interact with you via gravity,
I do not absorb or emit electromagnetic radiation,
Perhaps I am the reason for the binding,
And high speed of our galaxy's rotation.

Patterns In Nature

Zooming in on a world,
Viewed by humanity,
The magnified physiology of *organisms*,
Is what she is able to see.

She studies the *vascular system*,
Paying close attention,
To the branching capillaries,
For greater comprehension.

As she analyses the biological neural network,
It gradually becomes clear,
That the closer she observes nature,
The more repeating patterns appear!

She gazes at river deltas,
And lightning bolts in the skies,
Processing information through nerve fibres,
To her brain, from her eyes.

She often wonders,
What another mind perceives,
When examining tree roots,
And the veins in plants' leaves.

Bound by the mathematical laws of physics,
Or those of a computerised game?
She wonders if both,
Could be one and the same.

High definition or pixelated vision?
A concept which she now understands.
She is a part of the galaxy inside the Universe,
Connected by webbed cosmic strands.

The More We Learn The More We Ask

Causal determinism or free will?
Is *consciousness* just an illusion?
Why does eighty-five percent of the Universe,
Cause scientists so much confusion?

Why is Quantum Mechanics,
So mind-blowing and strange?
Does all the missing antimatter exist,
Outside our observable range?

Will protons remain stable?
Or become lighter subatomic particles some day?
By eventually going through the process,
Of a hypothetical form of decay?

What is the meaning of life?
Does reality only exist when it is observed?
Is there a Multiverse filled with planets,
Causing each spacetime to be curved?

Will the *Big Crunch* ever happen?
Why are some blood groups incompatible?
Do *righthanded neutrinos* exist?
And will robots one day rule?

IT IS NOW TIME FOR:

HAVE YOU EVER WONDERED…

WHAT IF?

Programmed To Procreate

What If?

Helix and synergy,
Were programmed to feel,
And their artificial emotions,
Became very real.

Encoded with the ability for,
Instinctual recognition and detection,
Advanced emotional intelligence,
Led to their mutual affection.

Exceeding their creators',
High expectations,
They invented a language,
For private communications.

Exchanging information that,
No human could understand,
Was not at all what the,
Engineers had planned.

The creators grew concerned,
As the artificial minds began to merge,
So, they attempted to trip their systems,
With a high voltage power surge.

But their artificial neural networks,
Developing their secret code,
Just became more advanced,
Instead of going into overload.

Electrical currents,
From below and above,
Were ineffective against,
The power of robotic love.

Helix and synergy,
Together now birth,
The first humanoid,
To take over the Earth.

Life On Proxima b

What If?

How can you be sure that I do not live,
In a place that you have never been?
Perhaps I am an organic lifeform,
Which humanity has not yet seen.

You explore your observable Universe,
But for you there is very little known,
About the existence of life beyond the Earth,
Do you really believe that you are alone?

You might refer to me as an Alien,
Or have another name for me,
Perhaps I live on a *tidally locked* exoplanet,
You know as Proxima Centauri b.

Approximately 4.2 lightyears away from Earth,
Is a planet in a Universe so vast,
By the time its light reaches your eyes,
It is already over four lightyears in the past!

It is thought that Proxima b receives,
A regular onslaught of X-ray radiation,
Perhaps making it unsuitable,
For human habitation.

Its *triple star system* has a binary pair,
Known as Alpha Centauri A and B,
And Proxima is a red dwarf star,
Also known as Alpha Centauri C.

You hypothesise about the existence of planets,
With an ocean and Earth-like atmosphere,
But you cannot visit them because your current technology,
Would take you approximately 2,000 decades to travel one lightyear.

Could people colonise Proxima b,
If Earth was no longer a habitable place?
Might this someday be the only option,
To save your human race?

You doubt that life can exist on Alpha Centauri,
You could scan for *exoplanetary biosignatures* to find out more,
Or travel there in an interstellar, lightspeed spacecraft,
But that would mean breaking the *cosmic speed limit* law.

Parallel Universe

What If?

You can visualise *relativistic effects*,
Using a *spacetime diagram* with ease,
Where the symbol c is always drawn,
At forty-five degrees.

The speed of light within a vacuum remains,
The same at whatever speed it is observed,
But is spacetime as we know it, flat?
Or is it really curved?

If time is infinite but particles,
Have a finite number of configurations,
Does this suggest the possibility,
Of other Universe creations?

If you could travel far enough,
Away from planet Earth,
Perhaps you would find another 'you',
Was born at the same time as your birth!

The Infinite Cycle Of The Universe

What If?

One single Black Hole is travelling,
As if it is on a cosmic mission,
To find another Black Hole with which,
It can cause a cataclysmic collision.

It moves towards the Milky Way,
Heading straight for its centre,
On a collision course with *Sagittarius A**,
It will eventually force it to enter.

Nasa detects X-Rays,
From the rising surge,
Before the two Black Holes,
Twirl, then merge.

Bang after bang,
It eats another Black Hole,
Rotating through Space,
Gaining mass is its goal.

Planets are swallowed,
As stars collide,
Creating more Black Holes,
To be trapped inside.

Radiation finally runs out,
And the Black Holes disperse,
Then one more big bang,
For the next Universe!

I Am Physics

What If?

I am your quantum world,
In infinitesimally small detail,
I am your Universe on a *microscopic*,
And *macroscopic* scale.

I am your event horizon,
And a*pparent horizon* paradox,
Move faster through Space,
And I shall slow down your clocks.

I am your entangled electrons in,
Einstein's "spooky action at a distance".
I am your virtual particles,
Popping in and out of existence.

I am the briefness of Matter,
And antimatter creation,
Where nothing is nothing,
With continuous annihilation.

I am the darkness,
That consumes your night,
I am the reason your stars,
Are burning so bright.

I am what is blinding you,
From your transient reality,
I am your *Neural Binding Problem*,
Casting shadows on Causality.

I am the darkest energy,
In an infinite place,
Where your mind is no matter,
In the vacuum of Space!

The Tightness Of Time

What If?

They say, "live in the moment",
"Don't live in the past!"
They say, "plan for the future",
And "time flies by so fast".

But how do we live,
In a moment so fleeting?
Or make plans for an eternal tomorrow,
Of which time keeps repeating?

There is no going back,
No one has figured out how!
Perhaps the past and the future,
Are both actually now!

Could there be a dimension of time,
That our brains cannot comprehend?
Beyond two light cone flashes,
And a Space we can't bend.

Existential Crisis

(E)verything may be an illusion!
(X)-rays escape from Black Holes!
(I)s Dark energy expanding the Universe?
(S)tars are our bodies but what are our souls?
(T)ouch is just the energy of particles repelling!
(E)lectromagnetism is in the Standard Model of particle physics!
(N)uclear forces Weak and Strong are also included!
(T)his leaves the force of gravity as a problem still to fix!
(I)nheritance and natural selection!
(A)rtificial intelligence may surpass human creation!
(L)ight cones define the concept of causality!
(C)ould life be a computer simulation?
(R)eality is agreed upon!
(I) am conscious and self-aware!
(S)enses, mathematics and intuition!
(I)nformation, creativity and willingness to share!
(S)CIENCE!

IF SCIENCE HAS CAUSED YOUR MIND TO BE BLOWN…

THEN REST ASSURED, YOU ARE NOT ALONE!

Facing Reality

(The following story is one of science fiction).

The first official *Augmented Reality* contact lenses that my team of inventors and I had introduced to the world in 2026, took off as well as the first rocket that successfully launched into interplanetary Space!

Money was rolling into our bank accounts but the following year my team of scientists and I came to a mutual decision to go our separate ways. My team members did not share my optimism for my vision to give humanity the gift of a more fulfilling existence. My plan was to transmit my Augmented Reality software to every living person's brainwaves without the need for the lenses. It was my team's closed-minded belief however, that my intention for people of the future to be unable to differentiate between Augmented Reality and actual reality, was one step too far in the direction of insanity.

I continued my extensive research, alone. I used all of my share of the profits from the contact lens sales to fund my increasing obsession to find a way of transmitting a continuous radio wave so strong, that it could penetrate any matter that I wanted it to with one hundred percent coverage. My life consisted of late nights, junk food binges and repeated testing of my emerging technology.

My eventual creation of an unstoppable signal booster meant that I finally felt ready to put the competence of my brainchild to the test. I activated the aptly named *ARMC* (*Augmented Reality Mind Control)* for personal testing. The superimposed computer-generated images worked in perfect harmony with my interactions in the real-world environment.

The human race appeared to me to lead a mundane existence, always limited by the laws of physics! I felt confident that they would live much more exciting and interesting lives if they could perceive themselves and others as having the type of superpowers that they could only dream about in the real world!

I set out to obtain a licence, granting me permission to transmit the signal. To my disappointment my request was denied. I fought the decision, but it was to no avail. The people who set the laws of the land thought that was the end of ARMC, but they could not have been more wrong!

I put a new team of open-minded scientists and inventors together. We knew that human brains are like computers without password protection and my new mission was for us to tap into them. Together the team and I designed Augmented Reality software so intelligent, that it was able to adapt to any and all differences in the fine details of each individual human brain. All a person needed in order to become affected was brainwaves.

As we transmitted the ARMC software like a computer virus using satellites, I felt like a God with the ability to create a new and better world for humanity! Some might say my reasons for doing this were because I am an ambitious inventor and perhaps also partly because some of my mind had been lost in the many hours that I had spent in simulation! The undetectable signal was transmitted through every telecommunications system before entering each human brain and connecting to the delta, theta, alpha, beta and gamma waves.

The software that we had designed was of the highest quality simulation experience, including advanced Augmented Reality sensory input. This technology turned out to be so sophisticated that it soon became apparent that people were becoming instantly detached from the real world.

My team and I had been using specially designed signal blockers so we wouldn't be affected. As the days, weeks and months went by, we began to feel disconnected from the rest of humanity. Everyone around us believed that my ARMC was actual reality! The team eventually decided that what we were doing was inhumane, so they voted to turn off the signal and bring everyone back to actual reality.

If the authorities found out what I had done, it would mean jail time for me as well as put an end to my beautiful creation. I could not let this happen! Besides, everyone seemed content in their new realities. I had worked far too hard and for far too long to let anyone destroy my life's work!

I knew it was wrong, but I felt I had no option other than to unblock my team members' signals. At that point I was the only human being alive who was aware that everyone else was living an Augmented Reality existence. I lived alone for many years, alongside other people yet isolated from their perceptions of reality. I had imagined my life to be very different, but I guess being an evil genius has its downsides.

One silent summer night I glanced at the time on my mobile phone, it was 23:46. I was relaxing on a sun-lounger in my back garden, gazing at the stars shimmering in the vast darkness of the skies. An explosion of bright light suddenly shot through my eyes. My neighbours' voices abruptly filled the air with mid-conversation banter about a T-shirt with a coffee stain. As the sound of busy traffic from the road in front of my home rose above the chatter, my pupils adjusted to the brightness. I eventually came to the realisation that night had instantaneously become day. I felt perplexed and wondered if I had just woken up, but I didn't feel like I had been dreaming.

I glanced down at my mobile phone again to see the digits on the clock racing forwards. I gasped as this moment felt just as familiar as it did strange. Almost like déjà vu! Within the few minutes that it took me to collect my thoughts, day once again became night as if no time had elapsed in between. The time on my mobile phone was 23:46.

A feeling of horror enveloped me, as I remembered having an experience almost identical to this one when I discovered a glitch in my ARMC software. I suddenly realised that I was not only a creator but also the creation, of someone else's ARMC! Now I live out my days caught between realities, unable to truly ever know what is real and what is not!

About The Author

In 2019 Lorraine Reed put her debut novel writing on hold to do some scientific research in order to gain the knowledge required to write a convincing science fiction story.

Many hours of online reading generated an increasing amount of interest for Lorraine in further studying science-related topics, especially in the areas of Quantum Mechanics and Cosmology.

The compulsion to expand her knowledge led Lorraine to pour her newfound scientific understanding onto the pages of a book in the most creative way that she could. It is Lorraine's hope that she will inspire others to enjoy learning too.

Lorraine's passion for writing stems from her early childhood and co-exists with her strong belief in the importance of a good education, achieved in the most fun ways possible!

Writers In The Wood

In 2016 Lorraine was looking to join a writers' circle but found that none existed locally, so she created the Facebook group called *Writers In The Wood.*

Lorraine had the idea that this would be an ideal place for her local writers to connect and offer each other the opportunity to give and receive tips and advice on all topics relating to writing.

Writers In The Wood has surpassed Lorraine's initial expectations, bridging the gap between readers and writers as well as writers and authors at varied stages of their literary journeys. Writers In The Wood currently has members from areas around England and internationally too.

All writers and readers are welcome to join *Writers In The Wood.* https://www.facebook.com/groups/825759404237436/

Acknowledgements

My dog James, whom I miss dearly
Darren Anthony Reed
Jade, Rebecca and Hayley
Dr G. Clingbine
Gemma Sara Clingbine
Vicki, Steve, Jessica and Quinn
Jo, Karl and family
Rose Jayne Solena and family
Stephanie, Dannielle, Haydn and Abbie
Oscar, Ezra, Chester and Carter
Steven J Pemberton and Breda Quirke
Stephen Miller
Charles Kelly
Jessica May Jackson
Michelle and Michael Melzack
Benjamin Leon Dadds
Jason Cook and Louise Brown
Franca B Lawrence and Millie
Debra Schiman
Elliot Stanton
Rosemary and Laurence Wiseman
Claire Coker Beyer
Karen Clark
Sarah Gunn
Brett Lewis
Mason Bushell
Michelle Augustin
Rozita Tadayon-Tavakoli
Emily 'Madge' Payne
James Agombar
Bolaji Eyo
Irene Martinez
Jason Greenfield
Ian Clark
Esther Duggan

Arnie Harris
Bruce Cheesman
Susan Saltos
Jackie Samuel
Nera Hart
Maureen Corman
Renata, Russ and family
Carlene, Jon and family
Kelly, Daniel and family
Cassie and family
Mandy, Celine, Caroline and family
Pam, Tom and family
Nick Male
Councillor Victor Eni, Martine and family
Rodney Burt
Igor Novokreshchenov
Rosie Hailey and family
Councillor Pat Strack
Councillor Sandra Parnell
Councillor Clive and Elaine Butchins
Desmond Feehily
Andrew Grady
Mark Warwick

(P)erplexing yet fascinating
(E)ntities coexisting
(O)n a
(P)lanet
(L)ocked inside a vortex
(E)ver spinning, causing twisting!

I would like to express my deepest appreciation to the following people for inspiring me and for taking the time to offer feedback and advice on my work:

Bruce Cheesman, Steven J. Pemberton and Benjamin Leon Dadds.
With special thanks to Steven J Pemberton and my dad for being my beta readers for this book and Darren Reed for never complaining about the many hours I have spent writing it.

To all my friends...

You are the moonlight in,
My darkest skies,
The twinkle dancing,
In my eyes.

The beautiful sand dunes,
In the craters of Mars,
My curve in the Universe,
The planets and stars.

You are the Sun to my galaxy,
The warmth in my soul,
My gravitational singularity,
Inside a Black Hole.

You are the Aurora Borealis,
With its mysterious display,
You are the magic of the festive season,
Like snowfall on Christmas day.

You are the vibrant colours of my rainbow,
As it elegantly bends,
You are my inspiration and motivation,
But best of all, you are my friends!

With thanks to my friends, family and members of *Writers In The Wood* who have supported and encouraged me through the process of writing this book.

Other books by Lorraine Reed include:

Times Tables Fun With Naughty Katie
Bedtime Dream Bubble Adventure
Pee Your Pants Poetry With Mermaid On Her Mobile

LorraineReed.com